M000210756

GEMINI

THE ARTFUL ASTROLOGER

GEMINI

Lee Holloway

Gramercy Books
New York • Avenel

To my children

A Friedman Group Book

Copyright ©1993 by Michael Friedman Publishing Group
All rights reserved.

This 1993 edition is published by Gramercy Books,
distributed by Outlet Book Company, Inc.,
a Random House Company, 40 Engelhard Avenue,
Avenel, New Jersey 07001.

Printed and bound in Singapore

Library of Congress Cataloging–in–Publication Data

Holloway, Lee.
    The artful astrologer. Gemini / by Lee Holloway.
            p.   cm.
        ISBN 0-517-08249-7
        1. Gemini (Astrology)   I. Title.
    BF1727.25H65   1993
    133.5'2—dc20   93-24868
                                                    CIP

8 7 6 5 4 3 2 1

CONTENTS

Symbolic rendering of a seventeenth-century astrologer.

INTRODUCTION

Is astrology bunk, or is there something to it? If astrology is utter nonsense, why have so many of the world's finest thinkers, including Johannes Kepler, Copernicus, Isaac Newton, Carl Jung, and Goethe, turned to astrology for information and guidance over the centuries?

Some people may scoff when astrology is mentioned, but even these skeptics are usually inquisitive about their signs. Whenever I attend a dinner party, I ask the host not to mention that I am an astrologer—at least not until dessert—because the conversation invariably turns to astrolo-

In the middle ages, the wealthy consulted astrologers regularly.

gy. When people learn that I am an astrologer, they first try to get me to tell them about their signs and what lies in store for them. Then, in a subtle way, they bring up the next bit of business, which usually concerns a loved one. Finally, as you've probably guessed, they want to know whether the two signs get along.

We humans are an inquisitive lot—we are eager to learn more about our friends, family, lovers, and employers. Astrology is one way to satisfy that natural curiosity.

In the not too distant past, only royalty, heads of state, and the very rich consulted with astrologers; such consultation was a privilege of the elite. Today, astrology is a source of information and fascination for millions; astrological columns can be found in major newspapers and magazines all over the world.

Astrology is not a form of magic. It is a science. Put simply, it is a practical application of astronomy that links the stars and planets with our daily lives. A horoscope is a picture of the stars and planets at a given time, such as that of a person's birth. By examining each planet's position and the relationships of all of the planets to each other at a specific moment, an astrologer can determine your basic personality or predict a general course of events. Perhaps the noted Swiss psychologist Carl Jung summed up the concept of astrology best when he said, "Whatever is born or done at this moment, has the qualities of this moment in time." Astrologers form a continuous link with the past, and each human being, although unique, is part of nature and the universe.

Unfortunately, some people have the misconception that astrology dictates who they are and how their life has to be.

This chart dates back to fourteenth-century Italy. The inside circles represent the element, ruling body part, and orientation of each respective sign.

Medieval illuminated manuscript of biblical characters observing the stars.

Nothing could be further from the truth. Astrology does not remove our free will; it simply points out our basic nature and how we are likely to react in certain circumstances. Astrology indicates strengths and weaknesses, talents and abilities, difficulties and opportunities. It is always up to the individual to use this information, and to live his or her life accordingly, or to disregard it.

Like other sciences, astrology's origins date back thousands of years. There is evidence that primitive peoples recorded the phases of the Moon by carving notches on reindeer bones, and that they may have linked the Moon's movement with the tides, or the snow's melting in spring with the rising of the constellation now known as Aries. As early as 2000 B.C., astrologers were using instruments— carved out of granite or fashioned from brass or copper—to observe and calculate the positions of constellations. These calculations were surprisingly accurate, even by today's standards.

Over time, astrological calculations were refined and the planets were named. The Babylonians were the first to describe the natural zodiac, and their first horoscope dates back to 409 B.C. Centuries ago, people began to examine the stars' potential impact on human emotions, spirit, and intellect. Today, astrology is so deeply embedded in our culture and language that we rarely give it a second thought. The

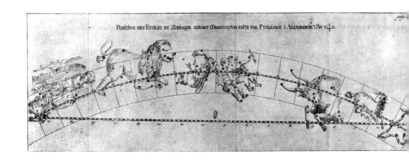

The twelve zodiacal constellations as drawn according to Ptolemy's descriptions.

days of the week , for example, have their roots in astrology. Sunday is derived from "Sun Day," Monday from "Moon Day," Tuesday from "Tiwe's Day," Wednesday from "Woden's Day," Thursday from "Thor's Day," Friday from "Frigga's Day," and Saturday from "Saturn's Day." Lunacy, which originally referred to so-called full-moon madness, now encompasses all varieties and forms of mental illness.

Before we begin, I'd like to touch upon one final point. Throughout this book, you'll see references to "rulers." A ruler, in astrological terms, has the same meaning as it does in human society; "ruler" refers to the planet that governs or co-governs an astrological sign (see pages 14–15) or to the constellation rising at the birth of a person or event. Everything has a moment of birth: people, places, profes-

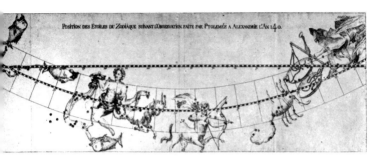

sions, even ideas; it would take volumes to show you what persons, places, and things your sign rules, but a small sampling has been included here. For example, different parts of the body have rulers, and that body part is often a point of strength and weakness. Gemstones and colors have also been assigned to each sign, although there are varying opinions about the validity of these less important areas. (It should also be noted here that the gemstone assigned to a particular sign does not correspond to the birthstone assigned to that month.) Generally, however, colors and gemstones are said to reflect the specific energy of each sign.

May *The Artful Astrologer* enlighten and entertain you.

Lee Holloway

THE PLANETS

The **SUN** symbolizes the life force that flows through everything. It rules the sign of Leo and represents ego, will, identity, and consciousness.

The **MOON** symbolizes emotions and personality. It rules the sign of Cancer and represents feeling, instinct, habit, childhood, mother, sensitivity, and receptivity.

MERCURY symbolizes the mind and communication. It rules the signs of Gemini and Virgo and represents thought, learning, communication, reason, speech, youth, and perception.

VENUS symbolizes love and attraction. It rules the signs of Taurus and Libra and represents harmony, values, pleasure, comfort, beauty, art, refinement, and balance.

MARS symbolizes action and drive. It rules the sign of Aries and represents energy, the sex drive, initiative, the ability to defend oneself, resilience, and conflict.

JUPITER symbolizes expansion and growth. It rules the sign of Sagittarius and represents higher thought and learning, principles, beliefs, optimism, abundance, idealism, and morals.

SATURN symbolizes universal law and reality. It rules the sign of Capricorn and represents structure, discipline, limitation, restriction, fear, authority figures, father, teachers, and time.

The nine planets that comprise our solar system: Mercury, Venus, Earth, Mars, Saturn, Jupiter, Uranus, Neptune, and Pluto.

URANUS symbolizes individuality and change. It rules the sign of Aquarius and represents intuition, genius, insight, reform, unconventionality, and freedom.

NEPTUNE symbolizes compassion and spirituality. It rules the sign of Pisces and represents the search for the divine, intuition, dreams, illusion, imagination, and confusion.

PLUTO symbolizes transformation and regeneration. It rules the sign of Scorpio and represents power, death and rebirth, the subconscious, elimination, obsession, and purging.

THE ZODIAC SIGNS

Just as there are twelve months in the year, there are twelve astrological signs in the zodiac. The word "zodiac" comes from the Greek *zoidiakos*, which means "circle of animals" and refers to a band of fixed stars that encircles the earth. The twelve signs are divided into four elements: fire, air, earth, and water. The three signs within an element share many similarities, but each sign in the zodiac is unique. The following section is a brief summary of the qualities of the signs born under each element. (The terms "positive" and "negative" as they are used here describe qualities, and are not judgments.)

The fire signs are Aries, Leo, and Sagittarius. They are termed positive and extroverted. They are warm, creative, outgoing, expressive, idealistic, inspirational, and enthusiastic.

The air signs are Gemini, Libra, and Aquarius. They are termed positive and extroverted. They are social, outgoing, objective, expressive, and intellectual.

The earth signs are Taurus, Virgo, and Capricorn. They are termed negative and introverted. They are practical, conservative, reserved, traditional, and deliberate.

The water signs are Cancer, Scorpio, and Pisces. They are termed negative and introverted. They are sensitive, emotional, imaginative, and intuitive.

The fire signs:

Aries   Leo   Sagittarius

The air signs:

Gemini   Libra   Aquarius

The earth signs:

Taurus   Virgo   Capricorn

The water signs:

Cancer   Scorpio   Pisces

G e m

Symbol: Twins

Planetary ruler: Mercury

Element: Air

Rules in the body: Arms

Day of the week: Wednesday

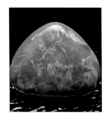

Gem: Opal

Color: Orange

Key words: I think

i n i

YOUR SUN SIGN PROFILE

I f you've ever watched an experiment with mercury, you know that when it is touched it scatters off into a dozen directions. Keep that image firmly in place, and you're well on your way toward understanding your own Gemini nature. Geminis are as fascinating and as unpredictable as mercury— and tend to run off in as many directions at once. Their motto is basically "so much to see, so little time," which accounts for their frequent tardiness. But Geminis aren't late because they're inconsiderate, it's just that they travel on a different clock than others do—and that clock seems to run either very quickly or very slowly. Geminis are also blessed with the gift of humor, which they frequently use to make amends if they offend others.

Because Geminis are ruled by Mercury, the fastest planet in our solar system and the mythological messenger of the gods, it's natural for them to keep up with the latest news and trends. They accomplish things at a dizzying pace and love to be in the know and on the go. Their abundant curiosity serves as a great asset for the role they were born to play: the purveyors of information. The realm of trivia belongs to the Twins.

Gemini's key words, "I think," reveal an approach to matters that is more intellectual than emotional. Geminis possess a dazzling intellect and a sparkling wit, and they can find the fun in every situation. They're forever young, thanks to Mercury, and they possess a captivating, childlike quality.

Geminis are well suited for many types of careers, as long as the work offers variety. There's only one problem: it can be difficult for Geminis to stay focused on a single job or project. With their quick and restless personality, they often suc-

Paul Gauguin

CITIES RULED BY GEMINI

Bruges, Belgium
Lombardy, Italy
London, England
Melbourne, Australia
Metz, France
Nuremberg, Germany
Rio de Janeiro, Brazil

A view of London's Westminster Abbey and Big Ben.

cessfully juggle two careers at once; a feat that most others couldn't handle comes naturally to them. Adaptability and versatility are innate traits that will serve you well as long as you don't scatter your energies too broadly.

Because Geminis are also blessed with the gift of gab, you really have an edge when it comes to communicating. In fact, you have the ability to talk others' ears off and probably often do. What else would you expect from a sign that rules talk, telephones, and travel? Consequently, Geminis excel in careers that require good communication skills, including writing, teaching, lecturing, selling, reporting, and radio or television broadcasting.

SOME PROFESSIONS RULED BY GEMINI

advertising executive
auto mechanic
broadcaster
bus driver
cab driver
canvasser
clerical worker
computer operator
editor
gas station owner
lecturer
librarian
literary critic
mechanical engineer
newspaper publisher
postal clerk
teacher
telephone operator
typesetter
writer

As for love and romance, Geminis thrive on diversity and get bored easily. This doesn't mean they won't settle down, but their passion for change can get them into hot water, for they often have many love affairs and may even marry more than once. This tendency toward being fickle is something you may have to work hard to overcome, although you may not

Isabella Rossellini

DOUBLE TAKE?

Isabella Rossellini and her sister Ingrid are the daughters of actress Ingrid Bergman and director Roberto Rossellini. As Gemini twins, they personify the symbol of their sign. Despite the obvious similarities, they are very different people. Isabella is a high-profile model and actress; Ingrid has avoided the public eye. Both women have been divorced, and each has one child, but Isabella is the mother of a girl, and Ingrid the mother of a boy.

become more consistent in romantic relationships until you are older. Because Geminis are always looking for something new to do or to learn, a relationship with you will most likely keep your partner hopping in one way or another.

Geminis approach relationships from an intellectual point of view, which is not surprising in a sign that typically wants to know how high the sky is or how many angels can stand on the head of a pin. This part-time comedian is not one for heavy emotional scenes; Gemini prefers constructive conversations about relationships. In fact, Geminis value being able to talk to someone—about anything and everything—above all else.

Judy Garland played serious and comic roles, danced, and sang, demonstrating her sign's love of variety.

Like every sign, Gemini has positive and negative attributes and the ability to choose which qualities to express. As a Gemini, you should be aware that if you don't demonstrate your best characteristics, others may see you as superficial and unreliable. As-suming you are a typical Gemini, it may be important for you to develop some restraint and resolve to say what you mean and mean what you say. Applying your incredible gift of reason to analyzing situations more carefully before you act or speak will go a long way in helping you achieve your goals.

ACTORS WHO
POSSESS THAT QUICK
GEMINI WIT

Danny Aiello
Jim Belushi
Morgan Freeman
Stan Laurel
Dean Martin
Marilyn Monroe
Laurence Olivier
Jessica Tandy
Gene Wilder

John Goodman

COMPATIBILITY WITH THE OTHER SIGNS

I n nature, some elements are more compatible and blend more easily than others, like fire and air, and earth and water; the same holds true in astrology. Therefore, some astrological signs naturally interact more harmoniously than others.

The information in this section describes how Gemini tends to relate to other signs. It provides guidelines to the potential strengths and weaknesses of a relationship between two signs. But remember, these are only guidelines. In the final analysis, the choice is yours.

As an air sign, Gemini is most compatible with the other air signs, Libra and Aquarius. The natural rapport of the air signs stems from their emotional and intellectual similarities.

The fire signs Aries and Leo

> **GIFTS SURE TO PLEASE GEMINIS**
>
> Books of lists, trivia, and travel tips; brain twisters and puzzles; magic tricks; anything orange; magazine subscriptions; a surprise day trip

are also very favorable partners for Gemini. Although Sagittarius is a fire sign, it is Gemini's opposite in the zodiac, so the relationship would be a bit more challenging than one with the other fire signs. In nature "air fans fire, and fire warms air," and the same holds true in astrology. This is why air and fire signs are basically compatible.

TYPECASTING?

Sir Arthur Conan Doyle, a Gemini, created the character of Sherlock Holmes in his famous mystery novels. Basil Rathbone, also a Gemini, played Sherlock Holmes on film.

Paul McCartney (Gemini) and Linda McCartney (Libra) are a shining example of the great potential for harmony in a Gemini-Libra union. Married for over twenty years, the couple have four children and are very involved in each other's lives. As a Libra, Linda is the more partner-oriented of the pair, which seems to have enhanced the relationship. In fact, ever since the couple has been together, Linda has been involved in a great many of Paul's musical projects, so that they (and later, their family) could be together—even on tours. As a Gemini, Paul is easily bored, but Linda's various pursuits, including publishing her photography and a vegetarian cookbook, apparently capture his interest.

The earth signs—Taurus, Virgo, and Capricorn—are not as compatible with Gemini as the fire and air signs, for they tend to lack the spontaneity and sociability that attracts Gemini. Earth signs are more practical and introverted, need security, and might find it difficult to cope with Gemini's rather changeable nature.

The water signs—Cancer, Scorpio, and Pisces—also represent less suitable candidates for Gemini because of their basic elemental differences. Water signs tend to look at the world from a deeply emotional perspective, while Geminis clearly take an intellectual approach to matters.

LIBRA AND GEMINI

 Libra (September 23–October 22) and Gemini can be a spectacular pairing, because they both enjoy social situations, good conversation, and new experiences. But Libra needs to weigh and balance matters carefully before making final decisions, and Gemini makes several decisions and tries them all until one works. Libra is very concerned with appearances and has a natural sense of style and grace, while Gemini is more unconventional and doesn't care too much about what others think. Still, Libra can benefit from Gemini's lighter and more explorative approach to life, while Gemini might consider using his or her considerable imitative skills to acquire some of Libra's tact and diplomacy.

AQUARIUS AND GEMINI

Aquarius (January 20–February 18) and Gemini are also highly compatible. As the rebels of the zodiac, Aquarians are often involved in reform through some new social movement; Geminis are also quirky, for they march to the beat of their own drummer. The blending of their ruling planets, Mercury (communication) and Uranus (change), indicates the potential for an exciting relationship. These highly social signs usually make a popular twosome, as they often have had so many different experiences that others enjoy talking with them. Aquarius is forgetful, however, and Gemini has a terrific memory. Aquarius seeks the truth, and Gemini believes there are many truths. Despite these small differences, there is a strong natural affinity here.

FIRST WORD PROBABLY LEARNED BY A GEMINI

Why?

GEMINI AND GEMINI

Two Geminis can form a successful relationship because of their similar natures; it's easier to understand someone who is so much like yourself. The problems two Geminis face independently, however, are amplified when they join forces, making it hard to offset each other's shortcomings, namely, restlessness and a tendency to lack focus. Properly addressing these issues will help to secure a happy and stimulating pairing.

Prince

ARIES AND GEMINI

 Aries (March 21–April 20) and Gemini share a wonderful childlike quality and enthusiasm for life. Aries is a dynamic, take-charge sign, and Gemini is a highly adaptable sign that's ready to go on almost any Arian adventure. Both love to be out and about, to explore and experiment. Gemini can fuel Aries' enthusiasm with new ideas and perspectives, while Aries can help Gemini take important steps to achieve his or her goals. Overall, this is a good combination.

LEO AND GEMINI

 Leo (July 24–August 23) and Gemini make a good match, too. Enchanting Gemini lacks the stability and consistency that are Leo's strong qualities. Gemini, on the other hand, can bring new ideas and experiences into Leo's life, which translates into a lot of shared fun. One word of caution: if Gemini wants to enjoy Leo's warmth, devotion, and affection, Leo's need to be the center of his or her loved one's life must be recognized.

SAGITTARIUS AND GEMINI

 Sagittarius (November 22–December 21) opposes Gemini in the zodiac, and opposites often attract in astrology. Gemini is cool and objective, while

A good example of a Gemini-Leo combination is John F. Kennedy (Gemini) and Jacqueline Bouvier Kennedy (Leo). JFK was charming, youthful, and very witty (all Gemini attributes), and Jackie is dignified and has great style (Leo qualities). He charmed the world, and she won our hearts; together they returned a touch of glamour and a sense of drama to the White House. JFK's infidelities pointed up the difficulty Geminis sometimes face with commitment and consistency, but Jackie was an enduring steadfast Leo, so their relationship held together. These two were a sparkling example of how compatible this air-fire duo can be.

GEMINI WRITERS OF NOTE

Ralph Waldo Emerson
Ian Fleming
Allen Ginsburg
Dashiell Hammett
Thomas Hardy
Lillian Hellman
John Hersey
A.E. Housman
Robert Ludlum
Joyce Carol Oates
Alexander Pushkin
Salman Rushdie
Jean-Paul Sartre
Erich Segal
Maurice Sendak
Harriet Beecher Stowe
William Styron
Herman Wouk

Walt Whitman

Sagittarius is warm and emotional. Gemini loves trivia, and Sagittarius loves wisdom. Gemini wants to know things for the sake of knowing them, and Sagittarius wants to know how everything fits together in the big picture. This twosome can balance each other's energy if they can accept and adjust to their innate differences.

TAURUS AND GEMINI

 Taurus (April 21–May 21) could be described as the bedrock of the zodiac, and Gemini the butterfly. Taurus is methodical and practical, while Gemini whizzes through life at the speed of sound and functions from a theoretical standpoint. Gemini needs intellectual stimulation and loves to be on the go, while Taurus prefers quiet times at home and enjoys familiar people and places. The pairing of these two has inherent problems, but compromise could mean a successful union. After all, a night out trying something new could broaden Taurus' horizons, and Gemini certainly could use someone to care about the practicalities of life, like food and shelter.

VIRGO AND GEMINI

 Of all the earth signs, Virgo (August 24–September 22) has the most potential for harmony with Gemini, since these two share a ruling planet, Mercury. Virgo and Gemini are intellectual in their approach to matters, but that's where the similarity ends. Gemini loves to take chances, sometimes almost to the point of recklessness. Virgo is cautious, conservative, and conventional, and would find Gemini's frequent unreliability and changeability quite unsettling. Virgos take life literally, while Geminis make it up as they go along. These differences could be too trying for both parties, particularly as both signs tend toward nervousness. Many adjustments would have to be made for this pairing to endure.

CAPRICORN AND GEMINI

 A relationship between Capricorn (December 22–January 19) and Gemini is certainly an interesting mix. Because Capricorn is ruled by Saturn, the grim reaper of the zodiac, it's no wonder Capricorns are always saving for a rainy day and always expect the worst. Gemini, however, is ruled by Mercury, which is like being governed by a planetary Peter Pan. Consequently, Geminis are not big planners—they think all you have to do is "clap your hands if you believe" and everything will work out. This difference in attitude

FAMOUS GEMINIS WHO DIED BEFORE THEIR TIME

Judy Garland
John F. Kennedy

Marilyn Monroe

could cause friction. Capricorn certainly can stabilize Gemini's flightiness and help curb any rash behavior, but unfortunately this would make Gemini feel like a bird whose wings have been clipped. If both partners are committed to the relationship, they should keep these facts in mind—if they wish to be happy together.

CANCER AND GEMINI

 A union between Cancer (June 22–July 23) and Gemini poses many challenges. While Gemini has an aversion to heavy emotions, Cancer is as turbulent as the ocean. Gemini loves freedom, while Cancer is dependent and

Paula Abdul

GEMINIS WHO SING FOR THEIR SUPPER

Pat Boone
Judy Garland
Waylon Jennings
Al Jolson
Tom Jones
Gladys Knight
Peggy Lee
Barry Manilow
Paul McCartney
Lionel Richie
Beverly Sills
Nancy Sinatra

possessive. However, both signs are very restless, and even though the sign of Cancer rules the home, a Cancer uses his or her homestead mainly as a base of operation. Cancers like travel and adventure almost as much as Geminis, so this shared trait could benefit the relationship. Still, these two are so different that many concessions will need to be made in order to keep the relationship going.

SCORPIO AND GEMINI

Scorpio (October 23–November 21) and Gemini often come together, although this relationship is a blend of very different energies. Gemini's complex, changeable nature may intrigue Scorpio, who loves mystery. But Scorpio could also find this very same lack of consistency childish. Gemini, on the other hand, could benefit from Scorpio's tenacity and may be fascinated by his or her intense and deep nature. These two are very different souls, so if they do get together, they will probably make some strange music.

PISCES AND GEMINI

Pisces (February 19–March 20) and Gemini is not the easiest pairing. Gemini is logical, outgoing, and expressive. Pisces is gentle, emotional, and sometimes shy and evasive. Pisces' sensitive and worrisome nature could

Gemini Gene Wilder's quickness of mind, action, and speech are evidence that he is ruled by Mercury, the fastest planet in the solar system.

*The lyrics of Bob Dylan's music reflect
the ingenuity and perceptiveness of his sign.*

dampen Gemini's lighthearted spirit. Gemini's intellectual approach to life could seem too cool to vulnerable, dependent Pisces. This water-air combination holds many inherent and basic differences. This doesn't mean it's impossible for these two to get along, it just means they will have to make more adjustments than other astrological unions.

Remember, astrology's compatibility guidelines do not mean that one sign can't have a good relationship with another. They merely indicate areas where there is potential for harmony and areas that will require patience, adjustment, and acceptance.

BIRTHDAYS OF
FAMOUS GEMINIS

May 21

Harold Robbins • Judge Reinhold
Albrecht Dürer

May 22

Laurence Olivier • Arthur Conan Doyle
Richard Benjamin

Queen Victoria

May 23

Douglas Fairbanks, Sr. • Franz Mesmer • Artie Shaw • Joan Collins

May 24

Queen Victoria • Priscilla Presley • Bob Dylan

May 25

Miles Davis • Ralph Waldo Emerson
Robert Ludlum • Beverly Sills

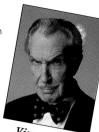

May 26

A. E. Housman • John Wayne • Peggy Lee
Sally K. Ride • Al Jolson • Hank Williams, Jr.

Priscilla Presley

Vincent Price

May 27

Dashiell Hammett • Isadora Duncan
Herman Wouk • Henry Kissinger • Vincent Price

May 28

Ian Fleming • Jim Thorpe • Gladys Knight • Sondra Locke

May 29

John F. Kennedy • Anthony Geary
Bob Hope • Al Unser, Sr.

May 30

Mel Blanc • Cornelia Otis Skinner
Benny Goodman

May 31

Brooke Shields • Clint Eastwood
Walt Whitman • Joe Namath

Brooke Shields

June 1

Morgan Freeman • Marilyn Monroe
Ron Wood •Nelson Riddle • Pat Boone

June 2

Marvin Hamlisch • Hedda Hopper • Pedro Guerrero
Thomas Hardy • Charlie Watts

June 3

Colleen Dewhurst • Jefferson Davis • Tony Curtis
Allen Ginsberg • Curtis Mayfield

Tony Curtis

June 4

Dennis Weaver • Michelle Phillips • Bruce Dern

June 5

Bill Moyers • Rosalind Russell • Richard Scarry • Tony Richardson

June 6

Alexander Pushkin • Nathan Hale • Bjorn Borg

June 7

Jessica Tandy • Paul Gauguin • Tom Jones • Prince

Tom Jones

June 8

Frank Lloyd Wright • Joan Rivers • Nancy Sinatra • James Darren

June 9

Jackie Mason • Cole Porter • Michael J. Fox
Peter the Great • Johnny Depp

June 10

Judy Garland • Frederick Loewe • Prince Philip
Maurice Sendak

Jackie Mason

Nancy Sinatra

June 11

Gene Wilder • William Styron • Jacques Cousteau • Vince Lombardi

June 12

Chick Corea • Jim Nabors • Uta Hagen

June 13

William Butler Yeats • Basil Rathbone • Ally Sheedy
Malcolm McDowell

June 14

Donald Trump • Steffi Graf • Harriet Beecher Stowe • Pierre Salinger

June 15

Harry Nilsson • Jim Belushi • Erik Erikson
Waylon Jennings • Saul Steinberg

June 16

Stan Laurel • Joyce Carol Oates • Erich Segal
Roberto Duran

Donald Trump

June 17

Igor Stravinsky • Dean Martin • M. C. Escher
Barry Manilow • John Hersey

June 18

Paul McCartney • Isabella and Ingrid Rossellini • Sammy Cahn

June 19

Lou Gehrig • Salman Rushdie
Kathleen Turner • Blaise Pascal • Paula Abdul

June 20

Errol Flynn • Lionel Richie • Lillian Hellman
Danny Aiello • John Goodman

Errol Flynn

June 21

Jean-Paul Sartre • Jane Russell
Prince William • Maureen Stapleton

ABOUT THE AUTHOR

Lee Holloway has been a practicing astrologer with an international clientele for more than fifteen years. The author of a series of comprehensive astrology engagement calendars, she has hosted her own television and radio programs, including her current show on KABC Talk Radio in Los Angeles. A Sagittarius and the mother of three, she lives in Woodland Hills, California.